Lord, Mold Me

Deus,

   I hope you enjoy reading
this as much as I enjoyed
writing it.

     Love,
      Marjorie,
       12/28/14

Hope all is well.

Lord, Mold Me

Marjorie Brame Bennett

To order additional copies of this book, contact:
Xlibris
1-888-795-4274
www.Xlibris.com
Orders@Xlibris.com
700284

Contents

Dedication

This book is dedicated to my dear friend Mary K. O'Neal, who, during my first three books, listened to every word of every poem I wrote. She was in relatively good health and was proud to be the first hearer of each. She always made complimentary evaluations and told me she never heard one of my poems that she did not like.

Mary's health declined since then and she is not able to communicate as independently by phone. However, most of my visitations find her in good spirits and ready for a "good argument". I wouldn't want it any other way.

Acknowledgements

To God, for giving me the concept of this book;

To My Sweetheart Husband, Robert for carrying the family assignments while I stayed stuck to the computer to write this book;

To my lifetime friend, Bessie Perry Bulluck, who motivated me as she insisted that I read almost every word to her and for her expressions each time of how much she was enjoying the book;

To Emmary Cotton, my sister by consent, who was my first to agree to proof/edit as I wrote;

To Lucky B. McKennie, my biological sister, sister in Christ and friend, for lending her expertise of multiple proofing cover page layout.

To Janyata Fraizer Worthy, who offered me her writing expertise and encouragement;

To Sylvia Ponder, who helped with proofing and editing;

To all my friends who helped me stay motivated by their expressions of eagerness and excitement about reading my short novel.

1. The Benefits of Adolescence

Little Rebecca Allen was born the third of four children in the small town of Oxfordtown, Georgia. She was a loving youngster who was taught by her parents, Joe, an elementary school principal and Lue, a stay-home mom, that if she put God first and a lot of hard work in everything, she could accomplish whatever she wanted in life. Rebecca's family was one that prayed together daily. She noticed that leading the grace at dinner was an event that had become competitive among her and her older brothers Jeffery, age 15 ½ Darryl, age 14, two years her senior and her younger sister, Joi, age 10.

When they were younger, Rebecca couldn't have been more than six, making her older brothers eight and nine, their competition took a humorous turn. Racing to the table, the rule was whoever got there first could lead the family in prayer for the meal. The children laughed and giggled excitedly as they ran. Rebecca, for the first time, finally outran her brothers and was given the privilege of prayer. She placed her hands together, cleared her throat and then there was complete silence. She could feel the stares of her big brothers looking at her. She'd put so much energy into running to the table that she'd forgotten to prepare what to say! Sheepishly, she had nothing to say to God. Her brother, Jeffery proudly took her turn.

Now Jeffery is too busy perfecting his basketball game and chasing the girls in his sophomore class that he doesn't have time for such pompous rituals. But everyone in the family knew before diving into the delicious meals prepared by Mom from the fresh fruits and vegetables grown by Dad, prayer was inevitable. Rebecca looked forward to being allowed to lead the prayer with her family at mealtime.

She was blessed with above average intelligence and aptitude and was not even aware of the level of this gift. With this in mind, she received daily support from her older brothers, as well as her parents, in preparing her school assignments from kindergarten through high school. In her twelfth year of age, Rebecca was of average weight and height and in good health. Her parents made sure she visited her pediatrician at least once annually. Good physical and mental health, personal hygiene and cleanliness were important to the Allens. They knew these qualities were important to please God, so, they must be good shepherds for their bodies.

Her organizational skills were extraordinary, but Rebecca did not realize this either. She was always worried about how she was going to accomplish daily goals. After a few software installations, the used computer Dad was able to buy from a major discount store, was an amazing attribute to all the Allen household, both for academic and personal needs. If Rebecca could just use the computer when her turn came around, she thought, that would make a big difference. "Only if I had my own computer", she often reminisced. Then in retrospect, she realized even having one to share was a blessing in itself. As she learned to use its applications, she found the calendar a great asset in reminding her of assignments, test dates, project due dates and a multitude of tasks that would have prevented her from reaching her target dates. Creating formulas for spreadsheets in her daily activities made most of her frustrations disappear.

One day Rebecca met her new seventh grade classmate, Juliette Perry, who was tall and lean with long, thick, black hair that covered her head and almost stopped parallel to her elbows. Juliette was very pretty, but needed much more confidence than she was showing. Since she was new at London Jeffreys High School (L. J. High), she was anxious to make new friends. Juliette carried a sadness in her eyes that suggested loneliness. It was not likely that she would attract many, so she was willing to accept one good friend. She felt other classmates may not like her because she was poor, which was reflected in her appearance, and her mom could not afford to buy clothes for her and her other two brothers like other kids wore. Rebecca often reminded her that clothes are not that important in life. She should be very happy that God gave her a beautiful face and a good brain. Additionally, the beautiful, thick, long black hair allowed her to stand out among every girl in their school. Hearing these positive attributes for the first time, Juliette's face gleamed like it had never gleamed before. Her posture even erected. She felt so pleased with herself and decided to hang around Rebecca more. From this day, Rebecca and Juliette became closer and closer.

Since they lived only a quarter of a mile apart, it was convenient to walk to school together. They would alternate homes to do their homework and always finished in time to have a few minutes to play one of their favorite word games, Perkquacky. They loved Perquackey, the game of word formation, using only the letters faced upward on the die poured out from the black plastic cup that came in the manufacturer's box. This game required quick thinking and an advanced vocabulary. Neither one wanted to lose from the opponent's challenge of a word not found in their overused, barely held together Scrabble dictionary.

2. The Bonding of a Friendship

One day Juliette was not at their agreed upon location to meet Rebecca to walk to school. After waiting several minutes, Rebecca knew she did not have time to go the Juliette's house and yet arrive at school on time, so she anxiously hurried on. She concluded Juliette had gone to school earlier but did not have time to call her to let her know.

Upon her arrival, she constantly took advantage of every opportunity to spot Juliette, including bumping into classmates and lockers, but to no avail. She sighed with comfort that she would see her in their math class at one o'clock and learn what had happened. Rebecca could not decide whether to be worried or angry that Juliette had not warned her of her absence. Much to her dismay, Juliette was not present for math either. This really alarmed Rebecca. As soon as her last class ended, she scooted out the school door as fast as her legs would carry her to find out the goings on of her new best friend.

When Rebecca arrived at the Perry's home, Dorothy, (Juliette's mom, a widow), opened the front door with a smile, yet a sadness in her eyes. Her appearance was not the neat, sparkling clean attire normally displayed. Rebecca suspected something was wrong. She told Rebecca that Juliette had missed school today because she had been awake the whole night before with a terrible cough. When she took her to emergency that morning, the doctor had admitted Juliette for tests to find a prognosis of the problem. Mrs. Perry was so worried that Juliette would not have the strength to fight off the inflammation and viruses in her system. Her appetite had not been up to par lately, and could cause her to be too weak.

Rebecca became saddened too, but she knew she could not let Mrs. Perry see it and she knew it was time for her to pray that God would heal her best friend's body. "Mrs. Perry, may I go with you when you go back to see Juliette? I know she would want me there with her.", Rebecca said. Mrs. Perry said, "Sure, Rebecca, you're probably right, you may go tomorrow after school. I will wait for you to come after school." Rebecca then asked if she could come in for a few minutes in hopes that she could say something to make Mrs. Perry feel better. And she did.

On her way home, Rebecca walked a lot slower than when going. She kept asking God what she could do to help her friend. She was not sure if He answered her, but she knew He heard her. She knew that He was with Juliette but was not sure of what the outcome would be.

Rebecca's mom saw her arrive from the back door. With her head dropped, she wondered what was going on in the mind of that unusually happy and upbeat child of hers. "What's up, 'Buttercup?'" (The name Lue called her when things looked down). Rebecca looked up at Mama with those "I need you" eyes. She composed her thoughts so she could tell Mama about Juliette's hospitalization and get permission to go with Mrs. Perry see Juliette the next day. Mama gave her a big squeezing hug then whispered, "Everything will be alright." Somehow, Rebecca was convinced that Mama knew what she was talking about.

It just so happened Mama had made Rebecca's favorite meal of fried chicken, mashed potatoes and gravy, steamed broccoli, and sautéed Granny Smith apples with hot buttermilk biscuits. The food smelled so good! Rebecca wanted to say the grace at this meal so she could include some words to let her family know of the plight that Juliette was experiencing. This way, she did not have to organize her words or her emotions to tell the story.

Her prayer began, "Lord, I thank you for the wonderful delicious meal you allowed Mama to cook. It smells so good. Will you please heal Juliette's body so she can be hungry enough to enjoy some of this tomorrow. Now bless this food and give me energy to go the hospital and help bring her home."

Everybody heard Rebecca, but no one asked any questions. They all understood; they knew how much she loved Juliette. Rebecca stirred in her food, but ate like a bird. It just did not taste the same. All she could think about was going to see her best friend tomorrow.

Tomorrow comes and Rebecca rises early so she can get the school day over and go to see Juliette. She arrived at the Perry's earlier than she and Juliette routinely did. "Are you ready, Mrs. Perry?" she asked. "Just as soon as Jason gets in from school. You know that boy always finds some reason to take a few minutes extra before coming home and doing his chores."

Only a few minutes passed when Jason darted into the front door. "Where have you been, my child?" challenged Mrs. Perry. Jason was happy to report his whereabouts. "You know, Mom, I had to stop to see Ms. McKennie, Juliette's homeroom teacher, to pick up her assignment for tomorrow. She would kill me if I forgot", he responded. Mrs. Perry gave him a hug and a kiss on the forehead, then patted him on the back, while acknowledging her pride. She told him to get two gingerbread cookies and a glass of milk, then do his homework and his daily chores. His big brother, Wesley, should be home from basketball practice in less than an hour. She said, "I expect to be home before dark. Be sure to keep the doors locked. Don't let anybody in, and Mom loves you much!" Jason groaned to indicate he heard her but not necessarily to emphatically comply.

As the two headed to the hospital to see Juliette, Mrs. Perry took advantage of the opportunity to see where Rebecca's mind was focused. She initiated a conversation to employ Rebecca's feedback. Mrs. Perry began, "Well, Rebecca, what did you do in class today?" "Oh, the same ole stuff" resounded Rebecca. And we got our math test papers back. I got an "A"! That surprised me because I was not sure of some of my answers. I don't know what I would have done if Juliette had not studied with me. She has a knack for that stuff." Mrs. Perry smiled with an internal concurrence, "She has always been good with numbers." In order to give Rebecca a chance to equalize and express her scholastic strengths, Mrs. Perry continued, "Well, which subjects are you better in? I know you both like spelling." "Yes", Rebecca replied, 'we like spelling, but I really like Science and Biology. There is something about learning how God makes things work in so many areas not initiated by man just fascinates me. I cannot get enough of it, I think."

"Well, what about English, and History and Geography and Literature and foreign languages? They are subjects you will need later on in life?" "Oh, I do pretty decent in those, too. But they don't drive me the way Science and Biology do."

By now they have arrived at the hospital. Rebecca is cautioned to wait for Mrs. Perry because she will need to be accompanied by an adult in order to get to see Juliette.

As they enter the room, Juliette is in twilight. She realizes her mom's presence by the fragrance of her soap she'd used that morning. As she opens one eye, she sees her best friend standing at her feet. Mom's visit brings her joy and comfort; her best friend brings happiness and delight. "What are you doing here, Rebecca?" she murmurs with a smirk on her face. "Oh, I could not tolerate waiting for you to come home to see you." Then Rebecca begins to tell her how she felt the day before when she did not know why she did not show up to walk with her to school.

"It was difficult getting through the classes without knowing." she added. Then they began whispering, with frequent giggles, about the events they did not want Mrs. Perry to have privy to. Juliette said her coughs had subsided, and she felt a lot better. She could not wait to get back home to play some Perquackey. Rebecca reminded her she looked forward to that too, so they could break the tie and declare a champion for the "umpteenth" time.

Shortly, the evening nurse entered with a cheery smile asking Juliette how she was feeling. She could tell Juliette was much better just from the expression on her face. She told Mrs. Perry that from the results of all tests performed she would not be surprised if Juliette were dismissed the next day, but that was a decision to be made by her doctor.

From the sound of those words, Juliette sat up in the bed as she and Rebecca embraced each other with joy!

The doctor did dismiss Juliette the next day with instructions to resume normal activities, but not to over exert herself during the next seven days. Juliette knew this meant no soccer practice, no running to compete to see who would arrive at their meeting spot first, nor any participating this week in the volley ball game she loved during daily recess. Little did she know, her best friend would alter her own activities to avoid her having to be alone during out-of-class hours the school day. She learned that Rebecca was really a true friend.

This medical episode passed and Rebecca and Juliette got back to normal almost immediately, almost forgetting the scary event.

3. High School and College Prep

Years went by and they found themselves taking scholastic aptitude tests, college entrance exams and SAT's, attending meetings with counselors to determine what would best prepare them for entrance into the most reputable and prestigious colleges or universities. Time passed so quickly and there never seemed to be enough of it to accomplish all they wanted to accomplish. They were both still pleased about their friendship and were adamant about having become better students because of it. Now, they were hopeful they would get accepted to the same university.

Practically every high school girl has an experience with a schoolmate who tries to make life rough for them. It was easy to select Rebecca as a target since she was most popular, talented, smart and appeared to be already focused on her lifetime goals.

One day, while approaching her locker alone, Emma Tutt, a classmate who never impressed Rebecca enough to catch her attention, caught Rebecca by the arm hard enough to swerve her around, said, "What are you doing here, Class Nerd?" Rebecca was startled by the new title that she quickly asked Emma if she were speaking to her. "Of course', Emma replied, 'you are the only nerd around, aren't you?"

It was that response that caused Rebecca to realize this medium height, bulky female was making an attempt to intimidate her. Rebecca was savvy enough to know how NOT to respond to such a coward, so she took a deep breath and calmly stated, "You're the girl in my gym class. I heard some other kids saying how they admire you for hanging in there with your mom as well as you do since it requires so much sacrifice on your part. I agree with them because I don't know if I could endure such an assignment."

In the interim, Rebecca and Juliette had looked forward to their high school prom. They were equally anxious they would not have dates and would have to escort each other. Friendship is valuable, but they did not think they'd have to give up a prom date for the sake of friendship.

As luck would have it, Juliette just so happened to be in the principal's office the day twin boys, Melvyn and Delvyn Britt, enrolled in their school. They were tall, neat, handsome and whose charisma impressed Juliette. She was delighted when the principle suggested that she assist them to their class, since she was assigned the same class. For the first time in her life, Juliette realized she did not feel awkward being alone with the opposite sex, and two of them at that! The fact that they came in pairs must have given her a sense of security. As Juliette walked in making her introductions, she could see Rebecca through her peripheral vision; she saw the smirk on her face, therefore hoping to get a one-on-one introduction later. No time availed itself that day inasmuch as getting adjusted to a new school was more than a notion.

Weeks of observing Melvyn and Delvyn in classes and around the school gave opportunities for Juliette and Rebecca to assess their evaluation of where the boys' heads were. They were amazed at the intellect, exposure and self-assurance they brought. It seemed the girls made a simultaneous decision to get attention from them outside the classroom. After all, the Junior-Senior Prom was a few months away and no one had asked either one of them for a date.

Two weeks before the prom, Melvyn and Delvyn approached Juliette and Rebecca near their hallway lockers and asked to be their prom dates as though the girls were a package deal. For a moment, they did not know who was to be whose date, but it shortly became obvious that Melvyn would escort Rebecca and Delvyn would escort Juliette.

The girls had the time of their lives shopping for the most beautiful dresses in Oxfordtown. Rebecca asked Mom and Dad if they thought they could make a financial contribution toward a dress for Juliette. She knew Dad had planned something special for her and maybe he could subtract a portion of what he had planned to spend on her and apply it toward Juliette's dress. This would be a "God Send" for Juliette and Mrs. Perry. She had so many financial problems after her husband died although he had left enough inheritance to last a few years.

Mr. and Mrs. Allen had become very fond of Mrs. Perry and understood her financial struggles. They had, many times in the past looked for her needs whenever the opportunity arose.

Each day after school, the girls would walk to the mall in search for their dream dresses. So many of them appeared to have been similar to ones they'd heard other girls at school say theirs looked. Finally, there were two dresses hanging near each other in the last store, The Boutique, they entered that afternoon. Mrs. Allen had been such a supporting customer of the store since its inception. Her credit was good for whatever the girls wanted. Surprisingly, there were no two dresses like the others so each girl was attracted to her own different dress. They could not believe their eyes or their ears. Sprinting to the dressing rooms to test their choices, they entered separate spaces so they could have that private moment to discover the fitting of their chosen dream dress. Just like a movie, both girls pranced out of their dressing area to show off her dress to the other. They realized their timeliness, and giggled like any typical high school senior. Confirmations were made simply from their eyes, body language and the pleasure in the face of the sales clerk. Since Mrs. Allen had called ahead to the store, no transactions from the girls was necessary. They walked out with their dresses on their arms, snickering themselves almost into oblivion.

The high school prom was the highlight of the community and everybody was excited to watch the youth make their debut entrances and exits. Melvyn and Delvyn were ecstatic at the beauty of their dates. This was the first time Melvyn and Delvyn had had an opportunity to hold their lovely ladies in their arms without feeling out of place in a school atmosphere. "Wow, this is what I've been waiting for!" Melvyn whispered to Delvyn with a quick wink while Delvyn conquered with an under his breath giggle.

Everybody hated to see the night end. Both couples shared their delight of the evening and made promises to stay in touch.

Now that the most popular and envious social affair of the school year has ended, normality resumed and those daily assignments, study periods and competitions for grades were their routine. Every now and then, Rebecca and Juliette had an urge to take a break and take time out for leisure. Attending a school sport activity usually was an event they could budget in their schedule, especially since this gave them time to spend with Melvyn and Delvyn.

It was obvious that the twins need not worry about scholarships, and it was certain that they would be receiving many. On the other hand, Rebecca and Juliette never overlooked the need to guarantee their eligibility for the awards.

Nevertheless, they found themselves in the library daily researching the requirements of schools. They compared each schools' mission statements and the financial requirements for entry and networking to identify supporters and attain impressive referrals for academic recommendations. The BS program gives strong preparation for those wishing to attend professional or graduate school in biology or related disciplines, and it is also recommended for those who intended to enter the scientific workforce upon completion of a bachelor's degree. This criteria seems to be directed just right for what Rebecca thinks she wants to do. Thank God, they both should be receiving scholarships to sustain their financial assistance. Otherwise, they may not be able to attend their school of choice.

4. Off to College

The day finally came when they both received letters of acceptance to their choice school: Tuskegee University in Tuskegee, Alabama! Words could not express their joy! Rebecca was most proud because while she would be able to test her maturity and self-sufficiency, she would be in traveling proximity to go home every other month to validate that everything was going well in the home with the family. She could fill in all the missing updates about the goings on of her brother, Jeffery, as he awaited his responses from any college basketball coach to be assigned the play on their team. His dream was to play with the Vanderbilt University, but he would be honored to get an offer from the Duke University, The Ohio State University or Georgetown University. The time seemed to pass extremely slow as he checked all mediums of communications: emails, text messages and even went to the mailbox every day in hopes to tell Coach Roberts he had an offer from one of them. After all, Coach encouraged him for some time to practice and prepare for a professional career and with the knowledge, understanding, dribbling skills and shooting accuracy he had attained, he felt his being offered a position almost guaranteed.

There were so many freshmen arriving and excited to be in college. Some of them were happy because it was their first experience of feeling independence and would no longer be required to give an account to Mom or Dad; others were excited to start building a life for themselves toward a successful career. Examples had been set from their environments that created an overwhelming desire to prove to themselves they had what it took to excel. Rebecca and Juliette could not help but notice the "cute" boys interacting with them, but they remained determined to keep their focus on their reason for going to college. And besides, the they felt a loyalty to Melvyn and Delvyn.

Neither girl had finalized her area of concentration. They both had excelled academically, providing them multiple choices. Rebecca didn't have to think long about her decision because whatever she chose would have to be centered on Science or Biology. Juliette was likely to concentrate on Mathematics, and she did. They took every class they could together while completing their electives; once they began their areas of concentration, they would probably see each other only during their free time in the dorm since they were fortunate enough to be roommates.

5. Setting Priorities

Rebecca soon learned that she needed to develop stronger study habits than those she used in high school. After all, everybody knew everybody in high school and she benefited from the reputation of her older brothers or her past successes in maintaining a high GPA. College life is different and nobody knows her or cares about her past scholastic reputation. She is merely a number: a student ID number. At least no one knew what her final grades were unless she confided her ID to them. Of course, Juliette knew. They frequently checked one another's grades to save time. One thing that provided her strength was to show her parents how well she was matriculating throughout each semester. There was no way she would allow all the struggles Mom and Dad went through to give her the opportunity to attend Tuskegee University become null and void.

No college term is complete without extra-curricular activities. Rebecca decided to join a few: Debating Club, the Science Tutorial and the soccer team. None of these would monopolize her time because she had an innate talent for debating. Science was one of her main interests and she has been gathering data since early elementary school. The best part of these choices allowed Juliette to accompany her to the Debating Club meetings. Only having one primary debate per school year gave the both of them time for extended research and make unforgettable preparations.

Consequently, Rebecca and Juliette were fortunate enough to have attended the organizational meeting when officers were elected and the selection was made on what schools to debate. Topics for the debates were on the agenda. The head coach for the Debate Team encouraged the team to hold off on selecting the school until they received invitations announcing what topics they wanted to debate. Rebecca was elected President of the team and Juliette was elected secretary. What a coincidence! As they walked back to their dorm, many teammates shouted their approval of their being elected to their respected positions. Kristina, who was walking along with the debaters, invited Rebecca and Juliette to attend her Sunday morning worship service on Sunday. Since this is Wednesday, she felt this would give ample time for them to rearrange their study schedules to allow a little time to worship and establish a church relationship in their new hometown. They both accepted the invitation gracefully as they had been taught the importance of including God in their lives to help them through, not only the good times, but through those rough roads life can throw out. Shortly Rebecca, Juliette and a couple more girls from their dorm arrived home and each went to her respective room. The burst of energy resumed and Rebecca continued her efforts to get started on her next project.

6. The Academic Challenges Begin

The first day of class came on a Thursday, much faster than either girl anticipated; however, neither was overwhelmed. The classes were about the size of those they'd been used to at L. J. High and the professors were nice, yet a little less personal than they had experienced. Each professor gave an overview of what was to be expected: how each student could assure himself of reaching the goals, warning them that class attendance was not a mandate, but completions of assignments were inevitable if they expected to pass the course, and certainly to get a good grade. To Rebecca, every professor was "a piece of cake" with the exception of her Biology professor. "Can you believe this? Me, intimidated by a biology teacher!" she thought. "Well, we'll see."

By the end of the class when Professor Moreaux handed out the assignments for the next class, Rebecca caught a hint at what could become a challenging class for her. This challenge was just what she needed to get her adrenaline flowing. She hurried back to her room to start on the assignment. It was so easily done that she was in disbelief until it darned on her that the professor was probably just testing them to see where each student's aptitude lie. "Oh, this homework is really for Professor Moreaux's documentation to evaluate us. He probably won't even record these in our grade book', Rebecca sighed… 'or is this an opportunity for me to shine?"

No other class startled Rebecca as Biology did. She thought she knew exactly where to place her concentration because this is not like Mr. Lee's class when she was at L. J High. Rebecca studied so much that even Juliette encouraged her to take a breather from the books; mothering could tear her away, though.

Mid-terms were at her heels before she knew it. One could only imagine the anxiety Rebecca felt. She had not only a reputation at stake, but she was unsure if she could handle failure. That word was nowhere in her or her family's vocabulary. With this fear facing Rebecca, she spoke to Juliette about organizing a study group for the class. She was fortunate enough to have four girls to commit to the needed long hours of studying.

7. Spiritual Needs Met

Since they had committed to join Kristina for worship, an afternoon study session would be ideal.

Sunday morning comes and the four girls met Rebecca and Juliette in the dorm lobby and accompanied each other to the Reynolds Missionary Baptist Church. They arrived a few minutes early, so Kristina had an opportunity to introduce them to Pastor Curtis James and a few of her girlfriends.

As the worship began, they were pleased to hear many songs they sing in their church in Oxfordtown. As Rebecca heard Pastor James' sermon topic, "What is the Difference in Faith and Patience?" she sat up straight and became star struck in his presentation. The lesson that was written on her heart with indelible ink was an explanation of the comparison and/or contrast of the two.

Rev. James began his clarification with this soft spoken analogy: "Faith is an absolute belief in the word of God and His promise will protect us in all circumstances in our lives. Concurrently, faith is the substance of things hoped for, the evidence of things not seen.

Patience is the ability to withstand, to hold on firmly in your convictions—to persist against what appears to be adverse conditions." 'Don't misunderstand', he added, 'the amount of patience a person has is directly comparative to the amount of faith he has acquired. Patience and faith are inseparable; one cannot exist without the other. Since faith comes through hearing and hearing by the "Word of God, it develops patience and is attained the same way."

"The test of a person's faith', Rev. James, counseled, 'is in the Word of God which necessitates the use of the ability to endure and persist until the desired result is obtained."

This sermon gave Rebecca a lot to think about. She had never considered patience and faith as being the same or co-partners. She could not let go of this concept, and she knows she will be returning for additional sermons from Rev. James soon. This was the beginning of her four-year attendance of Reynolds Baptist Church.

8. Laborious Studying

It was easy to head to the library for their new study session. They toiled, sweated and strove in the wee hours of the morning. As always, Kristina bellowed out she was "starving!" Everybody knew this meant "local pancake house, here we come." The fifteen minute ride to the restaurant gave them another opportunity to extend their studies by playing the self-made Jeopardy game by describing a health condition and the condition had to be given in the form of a question. The first question was routinely an easy one to get everyone's confidence increased. Juliette initiated the game with the first question: "It causes a routine of sneezes, one after the other unannounced and when there is no evidence of a cold". Kristina's quick thinking and equally body flexibility allowed her the chime in with the answer, "What is hay fever?" Getting this one correct elated Kristina so she did not have to be as anxious to answer as many of the rest. She was certain the rest would be coming out strong!

No one but Rebecca was surprised that she passed with flying colors on her first test papers. "Wow, my studying and focusing actually did pay off. Maybe I won't have to go through this type of turmoil again. I will make my list of "Lessons Learned" from this first test.

By the time Rebecca and Juliette completed their first year, they had become pacesetters in their classes. For some, this may offer a time to retard the studying, but for these girls this only gave them additional energy. They knew every grade for every assignment, test and class stood alone. The only thing that mattered was the final and aggregate total. After all, they have three more years to prove themselves.

9. Summer Vacation

As the school year ended, Rebecca and Juliette were delighted to pack up and go back to Oxfordtown. As small as their hometown was, and the absence of multi-cultured residents and limited educational resources, it still had stolen their hearts and their loyalty. They will have twelve weeks to relax, yet incorporate enough studies to not become disconnected with their curriculum goals for college life. Rebecca was able to find a part-time job at L. J. High for its summer school session. This was a dream come true for her! So many days she sat in class daydreaming of what it would be like to be able to even tutor some of the students coming after her to build their knowledge, expertise and confidence enough to study the world of science.

Juliette pinned a job in the Accounting Department at the local bank. Her God-given talent in math afforded her an opportunity to make major contributions to the enhancement of the bank's financial statements and ledger sheets. Her supervisor, Ms. Garrett, was so impressed with her skills, she even suggested she come back during the Christmas break and they would be able to find a new task for her.

10. Sophomore Year

Their familiarity with the college campus, professors and many students made year two much easier than year one to complete registration and sign up for classes. The assignment of a new dorm was one of their best benefits because they were viewed as "upperclassmen". This was a change from all the hoopla brought on during freshmen orientation. However, remaining roommates also attributed to their comfort zone and allowed them to navigate through the daily requirements and activities. Electives were incomplete, but they were excited about getting closer to the end of the tunnel.

Since upperclassmen reported after the freshmen orientation, little time existed before daily classes began.

Rebecca has Professor Moreaux again. She is more confident than her freshman year. She felt so proud of all she has been able to learn and teach the students at L. J. High this summer that she knew she had a lot to build her own goals and aspirations and make not only herself proud, but her professors and her family and friends back home proud as well.

Every day was not always smooth sailing. Rebecca had just finished her most feared assignment for Professor Moreaux's 201 Biology Lab. She was charged to create a treatment for female skin rashes. One of her cousins, Pearl, back home, had been dealing with a rash on her abdomen for many years but since it gave her no physical pain, it was somewhat ignored. Rebecca tried on numerous occasions to convince Pearl to go to see her family practitioner, Dr. Horace, but Pearl always found a reason not to go or even call for counsel.

Now that Rebecca thinks she may have at least found a possible treatment to decrease the spread of the rash, she could not wait to present her sampling to Professor Moreaux. Her sample liquid ingredients allow the patient to apply small amounts onto the affected area after cleaning the skin with warm water, a soft, mild soap, then expose the skin to sunlight at least thirty minutes daily after the application and drink at least eight glasses of distilled water. Rebecca had even found a cloth that could be substituted as human skin and the sample interacted quite appropriately to support Rebecca's prognosis.

Upon awaking the morning her presentation was to be made, Rebecca had a friend to stop by her room with a laptop emergency and mistakenly used Rebecca's only piece of skin cloth sample to clean her laptop computer screen. Wiping the screen was stressful enough to cause an act of trauma for Rebecca, but her friend sprayed an old hair spray onto the computer screen. There was no time to run to the medical supply store to pick up another roll of cloth, so she had to convince Professor Moreaux to allow her to make her presentation at her next class meeting. Fortunately, Professor Moreaux had come to realize the efforts Rebecca always put in her assignments, so he trusted her honesty and allowed her to waive the presentation.

Sadly enough, Rebecca was very short on funds, so she had to borrow the money from Juliette in order to replace the damaged cloth. Juliette was quite willing to sacrifice the money for her friend. This type of frequent support has been what has brought them through thus far.

The next scheduled biology class seemed to have come quicker than the week indicated on the calendar. But nothing was going to impede Rebecca this time. She had enough materials left over to allow Professor Moreaux to do his own dry run test right there in the lab. He had become so impressed with the potential of the treatment that he just had to prove to himself that he understood the details of Rebecca's plan. Although he attempted to hide his enthusiasm via his notorious "poker face", it shone right through. He confessed his pride in Rebecca's creativity, detail of her plan and her energized presentation. Rebecca was convinced she had won him over.

One would think Rebecca would want to take a break and relax a few moments after that exhausting scare, but this only elevated her desire to get started on her next project. The only thing was, she was not quite sure she was totally mentally prepared to get started. So she had no choice but to calm herself long enough to map out her strategy.

11. Extra-Curricular Activities

Since Rebecca did not know how to completely relax, she would often phantom the idea of sitting in a movie theatre watching one of her favorite movies, *The* Great *Debaters, produced and directed by Ophrah Winfrey and Denzel Washington, respectively.* She could not spare movie money out of her scholarship allowance, so she borrowed a DVD from a member of her Debating Club. She spent many hours daydreaming of presenting her debates emulating Samantha Brooke, played by one of her favorite actresses, Jurnee Smollett. After all, she was just as smart as Samantha. Her repetitions of watching this movie always offered ideas for Rebecca in practicing on her deliveries. But she also was reminded that intellect is not the only quality required in becoming a great debater: Long hours of research, ability to interpret the perfect meanings at the perfect moment, reflecting the voice to make unforgettable memories, and most of all, stay ahead of the opponent. The more Rebecca watched, the more she could put herself in the role of Samantha, even in her class presentations. She considered that to be a huge asset.

Yet again, she felt lifted and esteemed after the movie, but she knew she had to resort back to her Biology class studies.

Concurrently, Juliette was independently preparing for her debate while multi-tasking her class assignments. She was enjoying some solitude in organizing her thoughts. "Everybody needs some quality downtime", she thought. Her overrun body caught up with her as she opened her eyes from an unplanned quickie nap. She submitted to the well needed R and R before regular bedtime. She had learned that going to bed extremely tired never produced a quality follow-up day.

After her brain and body had rested, once Rebecca arrived, she was able to engage into a decent conversation with her. But she was amazed, however, to find herself eager to go to bed and was making early preparations for it shortly. As always, Rebecca was babbling about how she enjoyed even the smallest details in the movie. Juliette moaned to indicate she was listening to Rebecca as though she had not heard this before. Juliette thought Rebecca seemed to need a repeat of watching the movie to reinsure herself of actions she could take and calm herself that her anticipated nervousness could be an asset in her ability to win the competitions. There was no way, however, she could even imply to her friend she was not interested in everything she wanted to share.

The next day the two girls decided to set up a schedule for researching data for their debates. They did not want to wait for the topics to be finalized before they had an action plan. Luckily they did, because Coach Aikens heard from Howard University and Morehouse College that same week. Two topics were up for consideration: "How Do College Students Excel While Playing a College Team Sport?" and "Why is a Four-Year College Degree Important to the Wealthy?" The girls were surprised at the recommended topics and realized they would require a mountainous amount of time to present.

They put their heads together surfing the internet: One statement got both their attention by reporting that "half the U.S. population lives in poverty or is of low income. On the contrary, some members of the U. S. population have earned an overwhelming figure of income. The educational level made a remarkable difference for most, but the exceptions including people with less than a four-year degree were earners of millions, causing a disparity in the processing of the accuracy of this site." This was only the beginning of their research, so they were eager to see more commentaries to prove their present mindset on the subject.

While surfing the internet in the library, Emma spotted them and decided to see how much turmoil she could bring on to circumvent their success. "So what are you nerds up to now? I bet you're looking for more ways to make some of us in your classes look even more stupid. We already know both of you are the favorites to all our professors. What more do you need?" Rebecca nor Juliette even raised their faces in response. This agitated Emma to become a little louder, accusing them of being too "high and mighty". By then, the librarian stepped over to warn Emma that her disturbance would not be tolerated. Emma looked at her with aggravated eyes, blew an animalistic sigh, but moved on while looking back at the girls as though she was not done with them yet.

The girls resumed their concentration on their research. They had so little time to make a lot of things happen.

12. Befriending Emma

Days passed and no sign of Emma. Suddenly one afternoon Rebecca and Juliette were walking back to the dorm after a long day of seminars. Neither one thought she had enough energy to endure the walk. Nevertheless, at only a couple of blocks from the dorm they just happened to see Emma seated on a bench, bent with her head between her legs, rocking side to side as though she could barely take her next breath. Rebecca paused long enough to verify that Emma was physically troubled. Her eyes showed a weakness and an indication of unhealthiness. "We cannot leave her in this condition, Juliette. Run over to the infirmary and see if a nurse is in. They can advise us on what to do."

Emma could hear Rebecca and saw Juliette respond hastily. The excruciating pain did not exempt Emma's hearing the girls' swift stimulus to rescue her in her most emergent moment.

The nurse seemed to have arrived in what appeared to have been seconds and was escorted by the school's ambulatory staff who quickly pulled out the gurney to transfer Emma onto. After a few preliminary questions to assess the problem, it was decided to get Emma to the nearest hospital emergency floor.

This was Emma's first admittance into a hospital and was naïve about what to expect. The list of routine questions asked did not provide enough data to make a prognosis, so the on-call doctor inevitable decided to admit Emma for overnight observations. She forgot all the attitudes expressed to Rebecca and Juliette and beckoned them not to leave her too quickly because she would not know what to do. Although they were not allowed to be in the room with her, just knowing they were accessible to her needs was comforting enough for Emma.

After several tests, it was determined that Emma had an erupted appendix and her arrival time at the hospital emergency was probably a lifesaver for her. Emma realized immediately that the two girls she had attacked so vehemently were the same two who may have just saved her life.

When she was released from the hospital after her surgery, she knew an apology was insufficient, yet, unescapable. Her opportunity arose one day while in the car of a classmate Rebecca and Juliette had convinced to carry Emma to her dorm.

Slowly Emma thought long and hard to put her words together well enough to express her true feelings of gratitude without embarrassing herself. She softly began, "Girls, I don't know how to say this to you other than I am so sorry I mistook who you really are. You see, I have never met anybody like you who would go out of their way to help someone, especially someone like me who had done nothing but be mean to them. My experience has taught me to get them before they get me. I suppose I concluded too fast you were just like those others back home and I wanted to get a jump start on you. The doctor said I may be dead if you had not gotten me to the hospital by the time you did. I guess I owe you a little something, huh? Can you forgive me?" The girls looked at each other, but nodded in agreement, saying, "There is nothing to forgive. You just be sure you have time to be kind to others you meet. You'll never know what can be the result of that." Emma agreed as she slowly exited the vehicle.

13. The Priority of Classwork

Nothing could be urgent enough to keep Rebecca and Juliette out of bed even in midday! Four hours lapsed before either was coherent enough to rise and resume their studies. Once they did arise, each moved energetically through the day as their satisfaction of helping to save someone's life enveloped them and remained in the back of their brains.

Rebecca stopped by Dr. Moreaux's class to confirm her next assignment. This new assignment was an easy one, but she was fortunate to be in his office at that particular moment and benefitted on seeing the upcoming assignment. It was not the intention of Dr. Moreaux to inform Rebecca, but once Rebecca saw some notes on his desk regarding Advanced Cures for the Common Cold, she became so interested that she could not avoid inquiring of the details in the directions this assignment would be going. "Doc.", she stated, 'I did not think there was any discoveries for curing the common cold. I would be so delighted to be a part of a team to discover and market this medical phenomenon! When can I get started?" Dr. Moreaux asked Rebecca to calm down and wait until he gave the assignment to the class. He said his negligence to place his papers in his attaché case allowed her to see highly confidential information. With that in mind, he would not want any hint that Rebecca had a head start on the rest of the class. It was then that Rebecca realized she was a little overly eager.

As she left Dr. Moreaux, she continued to daydream about her contribution to the assignment. She shared her excitement with Juliette who joined her in her glee. "Well, when are you going to get started?" Juliette chimed in. I don't know. Dr. Moreaux insists I wait until he notifies the class. I just hope I can last that long." Juliette, "You don't have to wait that long! Who is going to know what you are working on if you don't tell them?" Juliette asked. "Well, okay", Rebecca replied. They both resorted to their own personal focuses.

14. A New Emma

It is now Saturday afternoon when most students are trying to squeeze in some leisure activity to help them survive the next week. Rebecca, Juliette and a couple of other girlfriends were leaving the movies when they spotted Emma walking across campus alone. She looked weary with her head dropped. What's up, Emma?" One girl asked. "Oh, nothing". Emma said. "Just on my way to the corner store for some snacks. Want something?" "No thanks." they all replied, 'it's too close to dinner."

Well, we were wondering if you would be interested in attending church with us tomorrow." Rebecca asked. When Emma was slow to respond, Rebecca added, "Rev. James usually has a fruitful sermon to deliver. I always get something to bring back home. For instance, one Sunday he talked about loving your enemy. I have heard my parents talk about that all my life but it did not seep in until I heard Rev. James say it in his soft spoken way. And you know what else, Emma, I believe that sermon was what gave me and Juliette the incline and courage to help you that day we took you to the hospital."

"Well, if he can make that great a change in MY thinking, I suppose it may be a good idea for me to at least hear him once. What time should I be ready and where should I meet you?"

"In the lobby at 10:30 in the morning. It's only a ten minute walk, and that will get us there in time to introduce you to Rev. James before service starts." Rebecca affirmed.

"See you there. Don't be late. We are sure you will be glad you attended."

Surely, Emma joined the girls going to church at Reynolds Baptist. Rev. James greets Emma as though he had known her many years and delighted to see her return. Much to Emma's amazement, she also felt as though she had known Rev. James many years. He invited them to take their seats and promise to attend the following Sunday for their annual Church picnic. There could not have been a better invitation for either of them.

Rebecca pursued her interest in her research for a cure for the common cold, not without occasional interruptions by the thoughts of the church picnic though. After all, she had heard so much about the fantastic menu, the friendly competitions that would offer much repose from the routine hustle and bustle of her class demands.

15. Church Picnic

Sunday finally arrived and the girls were up early dressed in their casual attire. This felt so good to be able to go church in such comfortable outfits. Before they reached the church parking lot, they could smell a smorgasbord of aromas, see the sight of folding chairs and throw-away table cloths on every table, with a small bouquet of fresh flowers donated by the Deaconesses of the church and congregational attendees who appeared to have a greater excitement than they did.

Rebecca smiled in reflection of her memories of church picnic back home but on a smaller scale. Emma confessed she had never seen such a sight, let alone to be an active participant in one. She knew this was going to be a paramount of an experience. Obviously, there were people she had never seen at the regular church services, but she understood anyone wanting to be a part of this gala affair.

Just a few feet away, they saw Rev. James headed toward them. He seemed to always be available to greet them no matter how often they attended. They often wondered if Rev. James had college training in that area. No pastor had ever done it better.

As their eyes perused the church grounds, they could see several games set up for competitions. There were numerous board games, some old Maid cards for the children and much to the surprise of Rebecca and Juliette, there was a Perquacky game on one of the tables, supplied by Sister Banks' granddaughter. She seems to leave it at grandma's house assuring to have something to play when she visits. They would not have minded if no one knew how to play but them, but they figured someone must have known to have brought the game. There was a couple of girls who were experienced players and a couple more who wanted to learn the game they had heard so much about. It did not take long for the neophytes to learn so they were able to set up a small team competition to make the game even more fun.

About an hour later, they were invited to gather for grace and begin their indulging. "I have never tasted so many delicious dishes in one setting! I certainly hope someone will offer us a doggie bag to take back to our dorms. You know, this would be a wholesome study repast", Emma carried on. All Rebecca and Juliette could do was nod their heads in agreement. They never looked up as they repeatedly placed food into their mouths.

The girls returned to their dorms just as excited as they were when they went to church that morning.

Rebecca could not wait to update Mom and Dad on their unexpectedly wonderful feast of the day. Rebecca, speaking as though she was racing to tell the story first, shouted, "Mom, I always thought you were an excellent cook, but some of those dishes I tasted today are a "must have" for your recipe collection. Mom, I never tasted a squash casserole that delicious. There were flavors I am not sure I even recognized! There had to have been some Vidalia onions in it and you could not overlook the taste of the sharp cheddar cheese, maybe a little sour cream…uh! And the melting of all of them just awed my taste buds all day. I can still taste them! Juliette is on the phone now telling her mom how much she enjoyed the day also."

When Mom could inject a word, she was able to utter, "I'm glad you enjoyed it, Baby. Be sure to give Rev. James our love and thanks for mentoring you, as well as Juliette, the way he does. It really gives a parent peace, consolation and comfort knowing his/her child has such a spiritual being looking out for them. Give my love to Juliette too. Maybe Dad and I can take a Saturday afternoon soon to ride down and take you girls out, do whatever you would like to do to give you a break from all your studying."

While Rebecca was excited about seeing Mom and Dad, she just did not know what Saturday would have enough vacant time to allow Mom and Dad to feel their time was well invested in the trip. She knew the volunteering to come was based on their missing her so much.

16. Back to Normal

Monday morning came with the normal rush to get up and out for classes. The umbrella of joy and reminiscence of the previous day allowed both girls to move with prodigious attitudes and energy. Those incidences that usually aggravated them were smooth sailings. They even noticed positive changes in Emma as well. And Emma shared her change in attitude because of her experiences at church yesterday. She confessed that she knew she had a lot to learn and to change, but Rev. James made her feel it is doable and worth the effort. "I never thought I would be willing to make such drastic changes I think I am going to have to make." Emma confided. Rebecca and Juliette chimed quickly and simultaneously, "Yes, and we'll help you! They all chuckled and left for classes.

Nothing major happened in Rebecca's schedule today. She was tickled pink as she needed time for the transition of yesterday. Additionally, she had no way of knowing the dilemma Emma would encounter requiring their support.

17. Helping Emma Survive

Emma was told by the school counselor that she should change her major from Math to Finance based on the grades she had received up to that point. Emma could not understand the logic since they both required a gross amount of mathematics. Emma never viewed herself as a financier. She always thought of those people to come from a wealthy background with a global experience of how money works. And besides, Emma would now need to take courses she had bypassed semesters ago. "I don't know where I'll get the money for tuition for extra time and classes here. How can I tell my Mama she will need to borrow more money in order for me to graduate? She is barely surviving now"

"Well, you don't have to tell her yet", Rebecca said. Give me and Juliette a chance to think and pray about it. Among the three of us, we should be able to come up with something". Emma sighed, realizing again what wonderful friends she had been fortunate to have made.

In God's infinite wisdom, Rebecca ran into a graduate student, Elaine, who she had met earlier in the school year. Surprisingly, Elaine told her she was continuing her studies late because she had to change her major course work in her junior year. At first Elaine said she did not know how she could accomplish such a change so late in her coursework, but she was able to get into a work study program that provided money to pay her tuition and not have to worry her parents for additional financial support or having to borrow money to be repaid later. As Rebecca questioned Elaine on how she could be able to get into a work study program, Elaine gave her a website to browse. This website was passed on to Emma who found it to be quite promising.

Emma was approved and she began her job two weeks later. She was assigned to work in the office of the School of Veterinary Medicine to keep the utensils clean and track inventory. Although she could not imagine what talent *OR* knowledge she would bring to the table, she was just grateful to have found employment.

She found so many interesting objects, people, theories and ideas that before she knew it, she was making recommendations to her boss to initiate research he had never even considered.

Additionally, Emma figured this must be God's way of giving her that pet her mom could never afford during her childhood. There were so many choices that it never phased her to settle for only one; she had the best of many worlds. She could do the priorities of her boss and then play with the animal of choice according to her own mood for the day. *(Now it don't get no better than this!)*

Every day was more pleasant than the day before. She could not thank her girlfriends enough!

Now you would never imagine what sprigs were planted during this Veterinary experience. The following school year, Emma learned the budget in the School of Veterinary Medicine was cut; therefore, her position no longer existed. In just one week after being notified of the cut, Emma received a letter from a local hospital telling her that her reputation preceded her and their Children's School was offering her to do a little more extensive work with better compensation.

Emma figured it does not take the brain of a rocket scientist to figure out the benefits of this offer. She could not wait to share the good news with Rebecca and Juliette.

Emma could not understand her sudden change to being so spend-thrift. All her life Mom challenged her to be less eager to spend every dime she came across. But for this time, she could never think of anything to be a "must-have". Surely she figured this out. "God knew she would be financially wrought in her efforts to support her tuition and institutional costs. This was her first confirmation of God's role in her life's provisions.

Days passed as Emma delved into her newly granted position. She realized the blessing of her having this promotion came as a result of all the long hours and laborious efforts she put forth in the School of Veterinary Medicine. Who would have ever thought she would land a job in a hospital, working to make sick people better and feel better about themselves, *AND*, enjoying doing all these tasks at the same time. Most of her experiences with people's feelings were to make people feel intimidated and bad about themselves; until lately, those feelings were gone. In the back of her mind, she knew all these attitudinal changes result from her new self- esteem from Rebecca and Juliette.

Rebecca and Juliette have really made a difference in her life. They seemed to do good things for other people without having to put much thoughts into it. And Rebecca seemed to have that part mastered even a little better than Juliette could. This mindset seemed to always pull the best out of the most ridiculous situations they had ever seen. And before you knew everything was resolved, they were snickering, whispering and laughing out loud, then back to the books as if that were their ritual.

18. The Senior Year

It is now the beginning of the girls' junior year. Where did the time go? For Rebecca and Juliette, it seemed like only last year that they were all floating around not knowing anyone or anything, yet eager to see all they could maintain in their brains before the upperclassmen determined they were meager freshmen. Through moments of reflection, however, there were so many give-a-ways: always walking around looking at the scenery instead of looking at their paths of travel, examining the face of everyone that met, appearing intimidated by everyone and having to go places in groups of four or more.

The first year had passed so quickly, they not only had no need to dodge their upperclassmen, but they were upperclassman themselves. Nevertheless, they chose to use their year of experience to be big sisters to the incoming freshman class.

So many students learned of Rebecca's and Juliette's kind-heartedness that they became a large following by the Thanksgiving break. The students who were latecomers to the popular counsel brought in comparative experiences from the "not-so-nice" upperclassmen group and were convinced they needed to get to know Rebecca Allen and Juliette Perry, if only for escaping the dogmatic outcries for security. Little did Rebecca and Juliette know, they would become life-time friends.

Four years have never passed this quickly in their lives! Anxiety about being sure they had crossed all "T"s and dotted all "I"s seemed to be a daily question in both girls' minds.

Lots of calmness came into reality once the Dean of Academic Affairs notified them they have each been listed in the records of Who's Who Among American Colleges and Universities. Once getting over the shock, they called their parents to notify them and confirming that they had invested their hard earned money and time in providing financial support.

Mrs. Allen told Rebecca they had invited Mrs. Perry to join them for dinner to celebrate such a major achievement. Both girls hugged and sobbed on each other's shoulder to know their hard work had brought so much joy to their parents.

As always, the girls settled down to the real world and buckled down to the books so their reputations would not be tarnished in a matter of a few months and during their senior year. Rebecca accepted she could not dodge the Advanced Economics any longer. She liked using her laptop and never realized any need for further studies. After all, most of her friends were gurus at it and she faired pretty well with their assistance whenever the need arose. However, since this is a criterion for graduation, she thought she'd better buckle down.

19. Bonded For Life

Much to Rebecca's surprise, the coursework was a lot easier than expected. Soon she was able to do formats which she never realized to be so popular to the advanced computer users: She started off with personalized greeting cards, spreadsheets with formulas, PowerPoint presentations, newsletters and many, many more. Professor Johnson indicated all the applications may not ever come into fold, but so often the knowledge of one application is an automatic prerequisite to becoming an expert for others.

Another pleasant surprise was when Melvyn walked into the lab the second week of class. Missing a few days of class would not hamper his ability to mainstream since he'd had his own personal computer since high school. His enrollment to Rebecca, was a certainty for out-of-class tutoring; to Melvyn, it was an assurance to continue his relationship with Rebecca. Either reason was a satisfactory end to each of them.

This semester gave Rebecca and Melvyn the opportunity to really get to know each other intimately. Delvyn and Juliette were still an item, but there was no indication, yet, that a future together was in the making. Juliette showed no jealousy in Rebecca's blossoming plans. Since no marriage proposal had occurred, Juliette took the relationship as average.

20. A Proposal

By the time graduation came, Juliette had begun to notice a gleam in Rebecca's eyes even when Melvyn was nowhere near her. One day Juliette asked Rebecca, "What's going on with you and Melvyn? Is there something the two of you want to tell me?" With a shy smile and the dropping of her head as though she didn't know just how to answer the question, she replied "Well, last night Melvyn asked me to become his wife and I said YES!" as her voice escalated as she got closer to the end of the statement. Melvyn said he had driven to Oxfordtown a few weeks ago on his way back from one of the school trips. He had called Mom and Dad and asked if he could stop by to talk to them for a few minutes. He wanted to get Dad's blessings to marry me and made both Mom and Dad promise not to tell me of the trip. I should have known something was up because Melvyn had begun to act a little strange. But, please don't say anything to anyone yet. I have to tell my family I agreed to marry him." "Of course." Juliette whispered from excitement. "My lips are sealed! But it's best that you know now that I expect to be your Maid of Honor." Rebecca's smile and hug confirmed that Juliette would definitely be her Maid of Honor.

For the first time since college entrance, Rebecca faced difficulty staying focused on something other than academics. Each time she attempted to settle down to her studies, she would start reminiscing about her wedding date, the date most suitable for both families, whether to have the wedding in Oxfordtown or Tuskegee, the size of the wedding, including how many guests, what color scheme and décor she wanted, wondering how many guests Melvyn would need to invite, who she could get to make the best deal of a cake; the list just went on and on. She knew she needed Juliette's input, but she wanted her own thoughts to be a little more organized first.

She only lasted twenty-four hours before she could not survive this without Juliette. This was a dream for Juliette. They agreed to budget their study time a bit tighter to allow for wedding plans. It did not take long to determine whether to invite Emma, but did not want Emma to be a part of the decision-making. Emma was happy just getting updates.

21. Graduation, A New Beginning

Graduation day arose. Rebecca, Juliette, Melvyn and Delvyn were among the many students receiving academic awards. Melvyn had received a job offer at a fortune five hundred company over in Montgomery, Alabama. Delvyn had similar offers, but with his ROTC training he chose to enlist in the U. S. Air Force. He would be leaving for basic training in a couple of weeks. Rebecca chose a local job at a business in Tuskegee, Alabama to do medical research while she worked on her Master's Degree in Biology. Juliette received a job at Tuskegee University in the Mathematics Department.

In order to give Mr. and Mrs. Allen exhaling time and breathing room between graduation and wedding, Rebecca and Melvyn set a December 21 wedding date. This would also give them time to save money for her big day without having to depend on the financing from her parents. The plan provided a great time for everyone to exhale before sprinting off on the biggest event in the Allen family since the day Joe and Lue got married.

By the end of the six-month probationary periods on their jobs, Melvyn had received a twenty percent increase in salary and Rebecca had received a fifteen percent raise. Since these increases had not been in their budgets, they decided to open a joint savings account just for the wedding expenses. They did not have much time before their wedding date and they needed to pay off some of the debt they had already incurred. Rebecca started a savings account that required her to invest $100 per month and additional $1 was pulled out of her checking account and placed in her SavePlus account each time she used her automatic teller card. They were both ecstatic whenever viewing the growth of the savings in that account. They agreed on a small wedding and this appears to be a sure way of not going into a lot of debt for this one-day, three-hour affair.

Melvyn was performing top level at his job and enjoyed every minute of it. Rebecca was a high performer as well and she often wished she could send more money back home to help Mom and Dad with the tuition for her little sister Joi. However, she knew Mom and Dad appreciated everything she sent and they felt Joi would make up the shortage in scholarships.

When Rebecca and Juliette met for their weekly lunch date, they could barely allow each other to tell the highlights of their lives without interrupting. For the most part, the wedding updates were saved for last because it was too significant to have to wait until those things that could not be delayed. The greatest report yet was Rebecca's finding her dream wedding dress. And she found it on the right day, at the right store and at the right price. Can you believe that?

During their lunch conversation, Juliette surprised Rebecca with a recommendation of a wedding coordinator, Mrs. Veronica Weaver. "I hear she's the best in Tuskegee, Rebecca. And she looks out for new college graduates when determining her fees." "I can't ask for anything better!" Rebecca chimed in. "So when do I meet her?" Well, she just happens to have a free day this weekend, if that fits your schedule." Said Juliette. "Oh, that's great!" responded Rebecca. See if 11:00a.m. Saturday is suitable." They agreed and went on to discuss ordering her "Save the Date" cards. "Ah, this is so much fun." Juliette retorted to Rebecca. "Yes, it is, but it's also a lot of hard work. It keeps me anxious. I just wish I could convince Melvyn to give more input, but he just tells me to do whatever makes me happy; then he smirks and adds under his breath, "Just keep your happiness within our financial means."

A few moments after Rebecca returned from lunch, her cell phone rings. Her caller ID read Jeffery Britt. Rebecca recognized the caller ID and telephone number to be that of Melvyn's mom. Her voice squeaked as she uttered a weak and nervous, "Hello". The voice on the other end was soft, smiley toned and loving as she heard, "Is this Rebecca Allen?" By now a calmness had come over Rebecca and she gave a much stronger and warmer, "Yes!"

"Well, Darling, this is Delores Britt. I am so happy to get a chance to meet you by phone until we can meet face to face." For right now, I want to welcome you into the Britt family. (Rebecca's stomach sank with happiness along with about ten other emotions; she was not sure which they were, but she didn't want to give any of them up.) "Oh, it's my pleasure, Mrs. Britt. We should be meeting soon since the wedding is only a few months away. But Melvyn and Delvyn always speak so highly of you and the rest of your family, I feel I know you already."

"I know your parents are planning to finance your wedding, but is there anything the Britt family can do to take some load off you?" Mrs. Britt invited. "Now, don't be shy, I would not have made this call if we were not genuinely offering." she added to reassure Rebecca. After a short pause, Rebecca was able to reply, "Well, let me discuss this with Melvyn and get back to you. Is the weekend okay?" "Sure, my child, take your time. We know this is an important decision to me made." ended Mrs. Britt.

Rebecca thought that Mrs. Britt was even nicer than Melvyn and Delvyn had described. They established a communication that was pleasant for both of them: not intrusive, yet frequent enough to give each a comfort in their relationship. Rebecca had introduced her mom via telephone so the two ladies were often sharing ideas and laughter about their children as they matured into the young adults they had become. "Melvyn was so shy about dating, I thought studies were more important than girls. I don't know what Rebecca did or said to him, but I believe I noticed a change in him even before I realized the change was Rebecca", Mrs. Britt confided. "But Delvyn did date a few girls in high school although there was never a girl he indicated was that special one. And at that age, we were pleased." They both were heavy into their studies.

Mrs. Britt always reminded Mrs. Allen that whether it was a comical, dramatic, loving or angry situation, with the twins, she always got a double dose from them. That alone made the ladies laugh.

22. Wedding Plans

Rebecca and Melvyn tried their best to keep up with the schedule of wedding planning. "Thank God, we found Mrs. Weaver to be our coordinator. She has saved me so much time, frustration, money, and God knows what else!" Rebecca thought out loud. "I just don't know how I would make it without her" the thoughts continued.

Well, December arrived before she could blink her eyes, it seemed. Rebecca reviewed her checklist a couple times a day. Although she never found an incompletion on the list, she always thought of something she should have done, until Mrs. Weaver convinced her that no wedding plans for herself could survive her own critiquing. All Rebecca wanted was a day to remember for the rest of her life. After all, this will never happen to her again.

A day to remember was exactly what she got. The wedding was at Reynolds Missionary Baptist Church for convenience and to accommodate space to invite some of her schoolmates and professors. Her pastor, Rev. Robert Wheeler, from Oxfordtown, was invited to co-facilitate the ceremony. Each minister seemed to have been quite thrilled to be a part of this big day for Rebecca.

As weddings go, the ceremony seemed to have been over in five minutes, but not too quickly for the guests to observe the beauty of Rebecca in her petite custom made wedding gown for her perfectly figured body and the handsomeness of her 6' 2" groom, Melvyn, strolling nervously down the aisle to greet his prospective bride. The mighty attractiveness of the wedding party and what seemed to be a welcoming of both families in merging into one, created the warmest atmosphere the bride and groom could ever imagine.

Her reception was as elegant as any small gala one had ever witnessed. Mrs. Weaver had outshone herself in the decorations as well as the layout of the food. The small band selected was remarkable in playing the couple's favorite tunes. This was an affair to be remembered by all in attendance.

The couple chose to have a one-week honeymoon at this time because they could get more time because of the holiday season without using much vacation time. They were fortunate enough to get an excellent package through the local travel agency on a cruise to Paris,

France. Oh, what wonderful scenery! She never dreamed it to be so beautiful or that she'd be there this early in her life. She was impressed by the beautiful pictures taken with her new cell phone camera Delvyn had given them as a wedding gift. God had really been good to her as she thought she had done nothing to deserve such blessings.

Rebecca had intended to get souvenirs for so many friends and family; but she was not accounting for this to be during her honeymoon! Obviously, her plan did not materialize. She was able to pick up a few items for her immediate family, the in-laws and Juliette, though.

As we know, all good things come to an end. It was time to head back home. The flight was beautiful and there were two other honeymooning couples on board. While waiting to board their plane, it was nice to share and compare experiences about how they met and the many unexpected events occurring that almost sabotaged their weddings. In retrospect, they became comical incidents. They said their goodbyes at luggage pick-up with the normal promises to stay in touch. Each couple was too "into each other" to even think of anyone else.

By the time they returned home, Lue, Rebecca's mom had gone over, unpacked the gifts, organized the apartment and left little notes to help Rebecca find things as she started out as a new wife. Upon examining things, Rebecca was pleased and Melvyn was impressed.

It is Rebecca's first day at work since becoming *MRS. REBECCA A. BRITT*! She could barely get any work done due to the many co-workers attempting to inquire of every detail of the trip to Paris. After lunch, though she had to put up a "Do Not Disturb" sign on the front of her cubicle so she could at least determine and separate the urgent matters in the pile of papers awaiting her. As for most brides, concentration was difficult while her mind kept reflecting back to warm affections of Melvyn, the tasty food, the souvenir shops, the beautiful Parisian ladies who caused her a little envy and many more matters of minor credence. Rebecca's boss, Dr. Beverly stopped by to welcome her back and express she would give her a few days to get settled back into her routine before she would tighten the rope on her.

That was an unexpected gesture of compassion which made Rebecca work a little harder to meet all assignments.

23. Juliette and Delvyn Follow

On Rebecca's second week back to work and she felt she had settled back into her job routine, she got an early call from Juliette requesting to meet for coffee after work and before going home. The oddity of this request caused Rebecca to question the urgency. She asked, "What's wrong, Juliette? Is everything alright?" Oh, everything's fine." Juliette happily injected. I just have something to share that I want us to be face to face." "Well, okay, then." Rebecca declined. "I'll see you about 5:30 this afternoon"

As Rebecca drove up and parked in her favorite space, she could see Juliette at a window table. She hurried in to find out what the mystery meeting was all about. "Okay, I'm all ears! Rebecca expressed with excitement. Juliette could not begin talking for flaunting her uncontrollable grin. She starts, I know you have been wondering where Delvyn's and my relationship would go from here." Rebecca gave a slow "Uh huh." "Then you can stop wondering, Delvyn and I have set a wedding date for two weeks from now. He got a furlough from the Air Force and wants to get married and have a short honeymoon while he is off. We don't want to have a big to-do, just something small and intimate with a few family and friends. Can we have our ceremony on your patio?" "Sure Rebecca confirmed, 'but how are we going to get all the plans completed in less than two weeks?" "You see, Delvyn had been thinking about this ever since you and Melvyn got married and he and Melvyn have been secretly planning in the hopes that I would say yes."

Rebecca hugged Juliette in relief, but chuckled under her breath, wondering what Melvyn had to offer since he contributed so little to his own wedding. Juliette went on to say that Melvyn said he learned a lot from watching and listening to you as you made plans for yours. Additionally, Delvyn had a lot of dreams of his own, but never thought he would be implementing them so soon. She listened to his action plan and saw little need to add anything to it.

"I told Mom about it last night and she was thrilled for us. She always thought a lot of Delvyn, you know." Juliette summarized.

Juliette and Delvyn had the small ceremony they had planned and Delvyn, dreading to leave his new bride, was quickly on his way back to the Air Force. Juliette was saddened by his rapid departure but comforted that she had Rebecca to lean on as a friend.

Delvyn knew he could work hard and get promoted fast if he applied himself, and he did. In the interim, Melvyn and Rebecca looked out for his wife, Juliette and found her a nice cozy little home near them. She could not have been happier. The house note was small enough that she could easily make the payments and save the money Delvyn sent home for living expenses. This way, by the time Delvyn is discharged from Air Force, they would be able to purchase their dream home.

24. A Period of Health Challenges

Rebecca and Melvyn just celebrated their tenth wedding anniversary this weekend. Early one morning, Rebecca's telephone rang. This was not unusual because her boss would call on occasions to see if she could come in a little early or run an errand before coming in. This time, though, it was not Dr. Beverly; it was Juliette checking to see if she could ride with her to Oxfordtown to check on her mother. She did not need to stay long, but wanted to be able to see for herself how her mom was doing. Rebecca welcomed her; the company would be ideal. "Mom never complained, just shrugged it off as though it was nothing worth spending time worrying about.

When they arrived at Mrs. Perry's home, she greeted them with her warm and excited to see them expression. They were happy to see her, too, but it did not take long for Juliette to recognize that Mom was walking with a limp. "Why are you limping, Mom?" Juliette tried to ask without drawing too much attention to her concern. "What do you mean, Sweetheart?" was the reply. Juliette realized Mom actually was not aware she had a limp in her walk. That caused greater concern for Juliette. "Are you in pain?" Juliette continued. "Well, not right now, but sometime I have problems climbing several stairs at a time, but the doctor says it's just a minor case of degenerative arthritis.

Years passed and Mrs. Perry (Dorothy) was able to maintain her arthritic pain. Occasionally, she found difficulty doing chores around the house and yard that she had never had any difficulty doing before. She was still able to hold her secretarial position which allowed her to have a reasonably good health insurance. Her doctor's office was in walking distance from her job, so she found convenience in walking as well as realizing the stroll to the office was great for exercise. She knew that was just what all the documentation she had read encouraged. Frequent movement for arthritis patients is always effective.

After a few years went by, Dorothy's job became more and more stressful. The company had experienced many reorganizations resulting in multiple layoffs. She always seemed to escape termination because her performance spoke for itself. However, she felt the stress of not knowing when she may be affected in a layoff could be detrimental to her health.

She found herself frequently uttering a silent prayer, "Lord, please don't allow this job to cause me to be ill."

The day finally came when Dorothy resigned her job to start a small training business teaching young adults how to dress and to handle themselves on job interviews. She wanted time to organize her plan and gave herself a 90-day grace period to release much of her anxiety, make good impressions and also to ensure she had enough clients to give the business a great kickoff. She thought she could schedule a short vacation to visit her family back in Charleston, South Carolina before tying herself down to the unending workload she knew to be inevitable.

Little did she know, there would never be a consulting business; her problems were about to begin. After awakening one morning and standing to go to the bathroom, she discovered she could not move. She did not panic, but was terribly alarmed. After all, ten seconds is too long to stand, immobile and not knowing the cause.

That night as she lay in bed to fall asleep, she encountered a new predicament. Her knees felt as though there was no flesh on her bones to separate them. Only through her imagination did she determine this had to be the feeling of a skeleton when rubbing together. Coupled with the rubbing bones, her feet burned under the bottom as though they had stepped on hot ashes. Repeated visits to her family doctor continued and resulted in the same diagnosis of degenerative arthritis; his tone of voice implied the loss patience that Dorothy did not accept his diagnosis and that the loss of weight and exercise were the only treatments he could recommend. He advised her to go to a spa and do water aerobics. Dorothy knew her problem was beyond degenerative arthritis in her knees.

For several days, she contemplated going to a podiatrist. When she reached the point of intolerance, she made an appointment. Her doctor examined her feet and after getting Dorothy to answer a few questions, she wrote a prescription for the pain and one for the burning feet.

When Dorothy dressed for church that Sunday, she had reached her car when she was in awe that her feet no longer burned! The amazing part about this was she had not a shoe of any kind, not even a bedroom shoe, during the last several weeks, that were not painful by touch. She was in love with her podiatrist!

One night around the first week of July, Dorothy was driving home after a meeting. At one glance, she saw letters on a big neon type sign,

"Fit for Life Spa." Dorothy was elated to see the opening at this location much closer to home. It was too late to go to sign up that night so she went early the next norming. The cost to become a member was a little steep, but she did not allow cost to keep her from getting the relief she needed. The monthly membership payments could be drafted from her bank account, making timely payments a guarantee.

Dorothy was a bit shy, though, to wear her bathing suit at the spa. She was so sure other members would be judgmental of her overweight, out-of-shaped body. She had suffered so much pain by then that what others thought of her appearance was a minor chord. After getting into the pool a couple of weeks, she realized she had not noticed anyone either giving her any comments about her size or even making disapproving eye contact. Dorothy smiled to herself as she realized she may have placed too much importance on what people may observe. There were several members larger and more out of shape than she was. She never thought about her appearance again.

Long-term friendships were developed during her spa visits. They would create their own water aerobic exercises and remained in a cluster of a lane to chat. Most of the ladies were older than Dorothy, but they welcomed her with open arms.

She developed a diet that worked for her and was able to lose about fifteen pounds before Thanksgiving. She was pleased, but thought the amount of work she had put forth, two hours per day, six days per week, should have generated a greater weight loss.

No one suspected Dorothy to be in as much pain as she was because she was as active in her community and in her church as she ever was. Plus, how could a person carry an overflowing schedule as she did while bearing excruciating pain at the same time?

Rebecca was able to keep Dorothy supplied with the latest medical magazines on arthritis in the hopes that education would lead to a quick solution. Being informed gave her a sense of having some control over her body. She met a nutritionist at church who convinced her that proper diet would help the body heal itself. She was willing to do anything to remedy the pain she had been experiencing lately.

Her trips to the local spa became more fruitful by the day. It was surprising that she could eat as much and as often as she did and still lose weight. In a few weeks she began to notice how many improvements her body displayed just since she gave up sugar, fried foods, white-flour products, dairy products and processed foods. Putting freshly squeezed lemon in each glass of water resulted in surprisingly amazing improvements all over her body that she could have never imagined. Her gums were stronger and healthier; she was able to go to the dentist without being traumatized; after a few months, her ophthalmologist asked, "Mrs. Perry, have you been taking Chinese herbs?" (Her eyes had improved so significantly, he attributed it to the herbs); her finger nails were no longer brittle or easily broken; she was able for the first time in years to have her teeth cleaned without a shot to tolerate the pain (just for teeth cleaning!); her digestive track became simply a pleasant ordeal! There were so many other attributes Dorothy could not remember without writing them down.

The change in her eating life style also allowed her to shed enough pounds to return to the size she was when Juliette and Rebecca were in middle school. Additionally, she recognized that the pain she once endured was only present infrequently. She found herself telling her children how her need for pain medication had decreased since the beginning of her healthy lifestyle.

These changes were effective about six years. All of a sudden Dorothy experienced a new category of pain. This pain was even more disabling than ever. Her ability to do her exercise routine at the spa, to use her exercise bike or her elliptical machine in her basement or even to walk up and down stairs in her home became a most painful effort. Initially she thought the pains were temporary and would soon be a thing of the past. However, she realized every day warranted pain medication but she received little to no relief.

25. Dorothy Takes Charge of Her Health

When she had suffered as much as she was willing to take, she made another appointment with her family doctor, who, in essence, stated there was no cure for fibromyalgia. It was that moment that she realized he had no definitive plans for her. She sought to take her health into her own hands and was able to get an appointment with another doctor.

Dorothy arrived for the appointment for her new doctor. The trip was approximately forty miles from her home. This was a cold dreary day, affirming discomfort in itself to sit any time beyond twenty minutes. She was appalled at the length of time she had to wait before the doctor actually came in the examining room the see her. This was definitely a deal breaker. Also, the difficulty in getting referrals not initiated by that doctor to see specialists to diagnose her health issues was the solidifying stage in her efforts to move on. Dorothy was exasperated by the numerous phone calls she made, to no avail, with excuses for not being able to send the needed documents. She wanted a doctor she could trust with her healing.

Again, Dorothy left this appointment assured she needed to change Primary Care Physician (PCP) again! She shared her feelings with Rebecca. Before Rebecca could refer her, Dorothy had made an appointment with a new PCP. She was excited about an opportunity to find someone who would take enough interest to help her become pain free.

Her first visit with her new primary care doctor was impressive. He seemed thorough, willing to go beyond his specified responsibilities and addressed areas that later would be assigned to a specialists; gathered satisfactory historical medical data; requested X-rays be performed; prescribed medicines while explaining the effect and side effects of each.

One night Dorothy had attempted to drink the infamous liquid mix common for patients preparing for a colonoscopy. (This was a recommendation from her last doctor). After about two glasses of the mixture, she became so ill; the thought of the liquid made her nauseous. Her inability to sleep more than ten minutes at a time during the night (with frequent murmurs of prayer, "Lord, please help me!") provoked her to contact the gastroenterologist to cancel the appointment. As fate dictated, he recommended that she go the emergency room at a hospital close to her residence. She had a special, special male friend, Walter, who drove her to the hospital and other places she needed to go. She was so impressed with the speed in which she was registered then taken to a holding room for a doctor to check her out. Walter told the technician he was Dorothy's fiancée in order to be able to come in the back with her. It seemed at least three doctors and a nurses were in front of her in a matter of minutes probing her about her reason for being there.

When she explained her efforts to drink the liquid last night, a cute, young male nurse, named Justin came in to give her an examination and handed her a sixteen ounce container of a juice-type liquid to be swallowed as soon as she could. He would be back after lunch and do a follow up on its effect.

It seemed that Dorothy had only been in the emergency area less than thirty minutes when a doctor questioned if she knew a Rev. Kenneth. He could not be allowed back to see her without her permission. Dorothy replied with joy, "Oh, yes! That's my Pastor. Of course, I want him to come back!"

Dorothy was happy by now because all the pain had subsided. Nevertheless, she was disappointed because the on-call doctor indicated she would be admitted for overnight observation.

The overnight stay was so pleasant Dorothy could not believe she was admitted to the hospital. It was difficult to convince herself that she was not on vacation. The frequent entrances of nurses and other specialist throughout the night did not even bother her because they were so kind spirited.

A female employee entered the room, introduced herself as one of the hospital doctor's assistant, Ms. Birmingham, gave Dorothy a business card and asked if there were anything she needed. After the second time, Dorothy emphatically said, "Yes, is there a Primary Care Physician you can refer me to?" Before Ms. Birmingham could reply, another employee strolled in telling Dorothy she would be happy to schedule her an appointment. Dorothy nodded in agreement. Later, Dorothy was advised of her appointment to see a Dr. Arthur Morrow in four days.

Dorothy cleared with her insurance her date to see a new doctor. This would be the third one within the last four months.

When Dorothy updated Rebecca of her new doctor's appointment, Rebecca was elated for Dorothy because she had watched her struggle long enough.

Dorothy was impressed with Dr. Morrow, whose public relations demeanor was the best she'd ever witnessed in a doctor's office. She had never seen anything like it. He continued to impress her in the examining room with his unending questions to determine her needs and health status. Dr. Morrow was a young, highly intelligent, handsome, thorough doctor who made his patient feel he was going to do everything in his power to get to the bottom of their problem as quickly as possible. He asked all the questions the other doctors had asked and more. It just seemed that their personalities immediately clicked. Dorothy developed an immediate trust in his care.

One new route Dr. Morrow took was to refer Dorothy to go to outpatient physical therapy. This was the beginning of a pain breakthrough, she thought. The owner, Bryan, interviewed Dorothy to determine the approach he should use to treat her. After a few questions, she asked Dorothy if he could have her permission to use acupuncture on her. Dorothy replied, "Whatever methods you deem necessary to relieve me of this pain is fine with me." Dorothy made this decision blindly since she had never been given acupuncture needles before. However, in a couple days she temporarily mentally dismissed her mobile limitations and was moving around with no cane. She was cured for life, she thought!

As her treatments continued, Dorothy was assigned to one of Bryan's staff, Gina. Gina was a young, attractive, pleasant young lady who spoke with confidence of her knowledge of what Dorothy needed. She became Dorothy's biweekly therapist, but allowed Bryan to administer the acupuncture as needed. Before Dorothy knew it, she was disappointed any time Gina was not available for her.

Since Dr. Morrow worked out of the hospital, he had digital access to all of Dorothy's recent hospital medical records. He asked his nurse, Beverly, to make an appointment for her to see the Neurologist, Dr. Osborne, located at one of the local hospital offices.

26. A New Life for Dorothy

Dorothy's friend, Walter, after his unexpected outburst that he was Dorothy's fiancée, began to accept feelings he had denied before. While being Dorothy's transporter, he was privy to lots of medical info on Dorothy and began to evaluate the flow of her painful experiences. He knew he needed to make himself a permanent part of Dorothy's life so he knew just how to make that happen.

While driving to her next appointment, he took a long pause and deep breath to gather his nerves. He was eventually able to say, "Honey, you know I have been taking you to lots of appointments now, and I am just realizing all the suffering you have gone through, I don't want you to go through by yourself when there is so much I can do to help you through it. I know this is not a romantic way to ask this, but will you become my wife so I can take care of you? I may not be able to flourish you with material things, but one thing I am absolutely sure of is that I love you and want to do everything in my power to make your life as happy and pain free as humanly possible."

This was a proposal that caught Dorothy by an irresistible surprise. However, she did not need to think long about it and reached out to touch Walter's shoulder and presented him with a loving smile and a soft-spoken "Yes, yes I will marry you, Walter."

Walter exhaled and replied, I won't be telling a falsie this time when I tell the staff you are my fiancée." Dorothy leaned over and gave Walter a kiss at the corner of his lips. She felt that should last until they could do it properly.

Silence set in until they reached the doctor's office.

The receptionist received Dorothy and informed the nurse of her presence. Dorothy and Walter were allowed to wait in the examining room.

Dr. Osborne examined Dorothy's neck, shoulder, back and legs. He quizzed her about the pain and its location. Although Dorothy insisted the pain's home base was in her lower left hip, Dr. Osborne insisted its origin was the neck and shoulder. She could not convince him otherwise and concluded his bedside manner had a lot to be desired. Subsequently, he scheduled her an appointment for an MRI at the hospital lab the following week. Much to Dorothy's surprise, the receiving receptionist informed her the MRI would be performed on the neck and shoulder only and she would have to pay $200.00 out of pocket for the service. "What?" exclaimed Dorothy. She urged them to test her lower hip as well. The receptionist advised that only Dr. Osborne could authorize the change and if he did, she would have to pay an additional $200.00. Through her disgust, she telephoned Dr. Morrow in the hopes he would rescue her from the financial burden. Yet, she was told to go ahead and have the recommended MRI. She did as Dr. Morrow suggested.

27. Alert for Medical Procedures

About two weeks later, Dorothy received a telephone call informing her of an appointment scheduled to see a Dr. Mango to go over her test results. "Hum, she thought, 'why am I not seeing Dr. Osborne, since he was the requestor of the performed MRI?" However, she dismissed that thought and proceeded. Upon her arrival and stating her purpose for being there, she was taken to an examination room to wait for the nurse to see her. The nurse entered the room with perplexed words and body language. She said, Mrs. Perry, why were you sent to us? We are surgeons!" Dorothy could not offer any explanation beyond that she received a call to come at that time and she was there.

The nurse exited the room and shortly thereafter Dr. Mango entered with similar reactions as the nurse. Dorothy thought showing him the DVD would help explain her presence. He rejected her offer stating they had that DVD in his office. Dorothy and Walter made a quick eye contact with each other signifying they both had great misunderstandings.

Dorothy asked Dr. Mango if he could give her the results of the MRI. He quickly replied that there was no suggestion of shoulder/neck relativity. Of course, Dorothy had mixed emotions because her first thought was, "I told you so!" and the other thought was "I want my money back!"

It took a few weeks for Dorothy to calm down about the unwarranted test and expense. After all, she did not want to create any dissension between herself and the doctor who would have that much control over her health and her life. Walter offered little advice on this subject because he felt assured Dorothy would follow her mind and heart on the matter.

Each time she saw a different medical professional, she found herself going home googling to learn everything she could to become educated about her new diagnosis. Confusion set in when she had listened to the disparity of interpretation each professional gave regarding the same test results. The sad part about this is that some treatments were very expensive but none of the prescriptions took away the pain. After learning that none of the changes in different prescriptions for potent drugs was effective, Dr. Morrow just did not know what else he could do, so he referred Dorothy to Georgia Pain Clinic.

A couple of weeks later, Dorothy was scheduled to have the MRI on her lower left hip. Her ability to control her nervous system prevented the success of the MRI and required a repeat of the test after taking a medication about 30 minutes before redoing the MRI. Fortunately, this one was sufficient.

A month later, Dorothy had not received the results of the latest test. She did, however, have an appointment with Dr. Osborne to discuss another matter. He examined her and Dorothy observed unspoken concerns as he proceeded.

Walter began to ask the doctor questions too, after all, this is his future wife's health at hand. They both had begun to believe this doctor only focused on the dollar and not the healing of the patient.

At that time, Dorothy asked Dr. Osborne when he would discuss the results of the last MRI with her, he responded, "Oh, in a couple weeks." "What?" Dorothy replied with a quick add on, "You're joking, right? Dr. Osborne showed hint of a joke, but added, "I have not received the results of the MRI yet. Dorothy was in disbelief. It had been over thirty days ago! He should have received those results in forty-eight hours.

Little did Dorothy know that at her appointment two hours later with the Pain Clinic, the on-call doctor would walk in with the test results Dr. Osborne had just stated he had not received. She appreciated the warmth in the doctor's personality as he entered the room. He swiftly began to tell Dorothy that her condition required her to have spinal surgery. This was quite an unexpected recommendation. Her heart fell into her stomach! After a deep breath, she was able to softly articulate, "Spinal surgery is a *serious* surgery!" The doctor immediately agreed and advised her to get a second, third or fourth opinion, if she liked. What Dorothy gleaned from that statement was that he did not trust this advice either.

Dorothy placed the document in her purse that she had been given by the doctor. She wanted to wait until she got back into the car before she read it. Sensations took over and she forgot all about the document.

On her way home, she was going over in her mind how she would tell Juliette of the prognosis regarding the surgery. She smiled to herself with the satisfaction of telling her Walter had proposed that day and she said yes. She could tell that Juliette was distraught after hearing the update on spinal surgery, Juliette liked Walter a lot and could exhale in knowing how committed he was to her mom. She encouraged Juliette to keep the faith because she knew God would see her through this.

28. A Medical Breakthrough

The next morning, a dear friend, Mikayla, called Dorothy expressing guilt for not having checked on her recently. Dorothy encouraged Mikayla not to feel negligent because she knew she was loved. Then Dorothy began sharing the recommendation of the doctor on the previous day. Mikayla, counselled Dorothy with the good news of her own experience of back surgery a little over ten years ago. She said she willingly complied with her doctor's recommendation; the very day after her surgery, she felt like a brand new person. Later in the conversation Dorothy asked about any subsequent pain after the surgery. She said, "I have not had any! Dorothy felt Mikayla was her angel sent to rescue her. Dorothy emphatically injected, "I want the doctor you had! If his second opinion is that I do need the surgery, I want him to perform it!" Again, Dorothy googled Dr. Leon Kelsy over the internet and learned his credentials were impeccable! She knew then that God was cashing in to relieve her of her pain of multiple years.

Monday morning Dorothy was awake her usual before sunrise time. She had fallen asleep at the computer. Her eyes focused on the time at the bottom of the computer screen and she knew God had answered her prayer to not allow her to sleep beyond 9:00a.m.

When Dorothy called to make an appointment to see Dr. Kelsy, the receptionist reassured her they would take good care of her. From that moment on, Dorothy remained calm and was certain her worries were over.

A couple days lapsed before Dorothy realized she had not read the document in her purse. Once perusing it, she was amazed that spinal surgery had been recommended as the solution. The document made her even more eager to hear Dr. Kelsy's opinion. As he entered the room and greeted Dorothy, his first statement was, "I see you have been dealing with this issue a long time. Dorothy nodded with a smile. Surely, Dr. Kelsy was equally amazed at the interpretation of the results.

Dr. Kelsy examined Dorothy while having his nurse to record on a laptop his findings. He asked Dorothy to walk a few step for his view. Almost immediately he expressed with glee his recognition that her problem to be arthritis. He told Dorothy he wanted her to make an appointment to see one of his teammates who specialized in arthritis.

During his time with Dorothy, he repeatedly conveyed his failure to comprehend a referral to a spinal specialist based on the results he had just reviewed.

Dorothy was as pleased as punch just knowing she would not go through such a dangerous procedure. Additionally, she was excited to be able to travel on the cruise with her family as planned.

Her appointment with Dr. McDougal, Arthritis Specialist, went far better than expected. X-rays were taken and reviewed within fifteen minutes after completion. As most doctors will do, he showed her the X-ray results then advised Dorothy she needed total hip replacement surgery in both hips. 'Since the left hip is the worst one, it should be scheduled first. I will not tell you when to have the surgery, just that it is necessary. He allowed her to set the date for the operation. The procedure was scheduled for three weeks later, with plans to be housed at a rehab center for thirty days.

29. Dorothy Becomes Anew

Dorothy and Walter put their heads together to come up with an expedient plan. "Since we were going on the cruise in a couple weeks, this is a good time to get married and call the cruise our honeymoon." Walter said. Dorothy smiled admitting he had just expressed her thoughts. They had a small private wedding with a few close family and friends.

When discussing her discharge the day after her surgery, Dr. McDougal told Dorothy she was doing so well after her surgery, she would only need in-home rehab; a nurse would come into her home twice a week for three weeks. Consequently, her insurance would not approve her going to a center. She was given a booklet educating her about the surgery and a list of exercises with illustrations that she should perform between visits from the nurse.

Several days after being home, Dorothy was in awe when she learned she was taking the pain medication only fifty percent of the times the prescription allowed. This was phenomenal! She no longer needed the strong doses of medication.

Dorothy knew her prayers had been answered when she took a forty-five mile ride (eighty mile roundtrip) with Walter to purchase another pair of compression stockings for her swollen legs. The next day, Walter took her out to dinner. The ride to the steakhouse restaurant, coupled with the time she remained seated in the booth while dining, she was apprehensive about the pain she would endure once she arose from her seat. Past experience had confirmed that sitting that length of time would be a great detriment for her. As she raised her buttocks from the seat, she kept anticipating a pain that never came. Surely she thought it would appear on her way back to the car, but she remained pain free.

Sunday, Dorothy really wanted to attend church since their annual church conference was held immediately afterwards. From the time she left home and returned back home several hours later, much to her surprise, she felt not even as much pain as she had two weeks prior from having sat thirty minutes. Dorothy continued to hope God would allow her to understand the miracle she was experiencing, in addition to giving her a fantastic husband like Walter. However, she could not fight off the approaches from church members who felt she was too active too quickly and warned her of the danger she was placing herself in. Dorothy would just smile and share her actions were instructions from her doctor. Their expression of concern represented mountains of love, but she wanted to assure them she had her own interest at heart and would, by no means, jeopardize it.

Early one morning, Dorothy fell from her bed. As she was going down to the floor, she uttered a panicky prayer, "Lord, please don't let this fall cause a setback for me!" Walter panicky jumped up to rescue his bride. She convinced him that she was okay but thought as a safety measure, she called her nurse, Tameka, to go for a checkup to ensure she was accurate. She could not conceive the idea of going through more painful days like those she had gone through for the last year.

Luckily, she felt no more pain from that fall than she had from the prior days after her surgery. No damages showed on the X-Rays. As a matter of fact, the Physician's Assistant promoted her to resume her water aerobics, and said she was allowed to drive as long as she first made dry runs near her home and not get on the expressway.

She asked Dorothy if she would like out-patient physical therapy. Dorothy was tickled "pink" to resume that service. She walked out with an authorization slip for six weeks of bi-weekly sessions.

When Dorothy told Rebecca of her blessing for therapy, Rebecca told her she wished she could take credit for her blessing, but the PA had become a friend of hers and she was just a kindhearted, Christian young lady.

Dorothy shortly and happily resumed much of her routine as before surgery. She found herself washing dishes and other housework she could perform while seated, getting back into her schedule of choir rehearsals, Sunday School, driving short distances, going up and down the stairs in her home, and working on her computer longer periods than she was able prior to surgery. Although she was being rehabilitated at a rapid speed, there were times she felt it was taking FOREVER to get back to normal and even wonder if normal mobility would reenter her world.

Her therapist encouraged her to practice walking without the support of the cane or her walker. There was no way to determine the status of her progress. Sometime she could move speedily without support while other times she did not feel capable enough to go six feet without support. One good thing about her physical therapy was little mercy was granted her in requiring her to execute all the assigned exercises.

Since Bryan had strongly recommended that she not have the surgery on the right hip until the left was completely healed, Dorothy worked harder to ensure she did all she could to speed up the healing process. She knew the left hip would have to become the strength for the right as it has been for the left.

Weeks have passed now and Dorothy is becoming disappointed that she has not progressed as much as she had anticipated. She thought her progress would be further since her first few weeks seemed to have galloped to bring her back to normal. She had to be reminded that the doctor and the therapist still saw enormous progress.

Months passed and Dorothy had her right hip replacement surgery. As predicted, she was walking better that she had in years.

Each time Juliette and Rebecca came home, they marveled over the excitement of seeing Dorothy navigate like years before.

Juliette was so pleased that her mom had married Walter because she could not imagine her having found a better husband. She knew Mom wanted a man just like Walter.

30. A New Life Comes

Rebecca and Melvyn were ecstatic to share their good news of pregnancy. Lue, Rebecca's mom thought for a while she would never hear such good news. Mrs. Britt did all she could to hide her true feelings, but she could not fool Melvyn. He knew his mom too well.

Concurrently, Rebecca was so thankful to God that he molded her life to become Youth Director of Reynolds Baptist Church. She had realized she had talents to pass on to the youth that could shape their lives as much as Reverend James has shaped hers. They had such great potentials among them. She promised God that she would exalt His name in every way she could. The youth adored her and she knew her opportunities were God-sent. She was in training for her own child as she groomed those whose lives were already in her mist. She was proud to have Juliette and Emma on her committee.

31. Thank You Lord, for Molding Me

As often as they found time in their busy schedules, Rebecca and Melvyn prayed prayers of gratitude for God having orchestrated their lives as He did. No prayer ended without Rebecca thanking God for all the blessings in her life: her loving, devoted, protective parents who sought every means possible to provide for her and her siblings so they could become responsible productive adults; for placing Juliette in her life and for creating the best friendship one could conceive; for giving her the aptitude to matriculate in one of the finest colleges in America; for sending her the perfect husband with whom to spend the rest of her life, but most of all, for molding her in His image to be a friend to mankind according to His will.

She knew that God had supplied her and Melvyn the tools and resources to be good parent as each of them had experienced. What an orchestrator He is! To God Be the Glory!

CPSIA information can be obtained at www.ICGtesting.com
Printed in the USA
LVOW11s2347191214

419660LV00002B/122/P

9 781503 518964